GHOSTS
& GOBLINS

BY SUE HAMILTON

Published by ABDO Publishing Company, 4940 Viking Drive, Suite 622, Edina, Minnesota 55435.
Copyright ©2007 by Abdo Consulting Group, Inc. International copyrights reserved in all countries.
No part of this book may be reproduced in any form without written permission from the publisher.
ABDO & Daughters™ is a trademark and logo of ABDO Publishing Company.

Printed in the United States.

Editors: John Hamilton/Tad Bornhoft
Graphic Design: Sue Hamilton
Cover Design: Neil Klinepier
Cover Illustration: *Fault Lines* ©1997 Don Maitz
Interior Photos and Illustrations: p 1 Detail of *Ghostslayer*, ©1980 Don Maitz; pp 4-5 *Nightmare Ghost*, ©1977 Don Maitz; p 6 The Brown Lady of Raynham Hall, Captain Provand and Indre Shira; p 7 *Ghostslayer*, ©1980 Don Maitz; p 8 World War I squadron, Royal Air Force; p 8 Spirit photo of Mary Todd/Abraham Lincoln, William Mumler; p 9 *Lincoln's Last Day* by Howard Pyle, Mary Evans; p 10 Willie Lincoln, courtesy Chicago Historical Society; p 11 *Fault Lines*, ©1997 Don Maitz; pg 12 Fox family, Mary Evans; pg 13 Fox sisters, Mary Evans; pg 14 Toys "R" Us logo, courtesy Toys "R" Us; pg 15 (top) The Bell house, courtesy the Bell family; (bottom) Carney Bell, AP/Wideworld; p 16 Foggy lane behind the University of Toronto, courtesy Archives of Ontario; p 17 *Dispell Magic*, ©1995 Don Maitz; p 18 (top) Sarah Winchester and (bottom) Tower, courtesy Winchester Mystery House, San Jose, CA; p 19 (top) Stairs to ceiling and (bottom) Outside view of the Winchester house, courtesy Winchester Mystery House, San Jose, CA; p 20 *Queen Mary* with longshoremen waving, Corbis; p 21 (top) *Queen Mary* docked, AP/Wideworld; (bottom) USS *Hornet*, AP/Wideworld; p 22 Johnny Checketts in his Spitfire, AP/Wideworld; p 23 Continental Airlines jet, Corbis; p 24 *Ghostbusters* movie image, courtesy Columbia Pictures; p 25 Andrew Green, Corbis; p 27 James Randi, Corbis; p 28 Goblin, Mary Evans; p 29 *Horned King*, ©1976 Don Maitz; p 32 *Grim Reaper in Purgatory*, ©1980 Don Maitz

Library of Congress Cataloging-in-Publication Data

Hamilton, Sue L., 1959-
 Ghosts & goblins / Sue Hamilton.
  p. cm. -- (The world of horror)
 Includes index.
 ISBN-13: 978-1-59928-767-6
 ISBN-10: 1-59928-767-6
 1. Ghosts--Juvenile literature. 2. Goblins--Juvenile literature. I. Title. II. Title: Ghosts and globlins.

BF1461.H296 2007
133.1--dc22
                          2006032735

CONTENTS

COAST-TO-COAST GHOSTS

Did you just feel something? A cool, moist Popsicle wind? Did you see that? As you get up for a late-night trip to the bathroom, your sleep-encased head turns at a slight movement. A wispy snow-shadow disappears down the hall. Did you hear that? It sounded like a soft moan, like a student with lots of homework. At first you think it might be the wind, but then you realize it's dead still outside.

For centuries, tales of the deceased appearing before the living have haunted the world. Ghosts are defined as the spirits of people who have died. But the form they take varies greatly. They may appear as a shadowy presence or they may be invisible. They may never make a sound or they may moan, howl, and knock over objects. Some are good. Some are thought to be evil.

Most spirits seem to have unfinished business here on Earth. Some had tragic lives that ended too soon, or violently—a drowning or an auto accident. They may have been murdered. They may have committed suicide. By killing themselves, are their spirits unable to leave the Earthly realm?

Around the world, from continent to continent, coast to coast, ghost stories are plentiful. But are these specters real? Or are they the result of over-active human imaginations? You decide.

Above: Nightmare Ghost by Don Maitz.

Famous Phantoms

Ghost sightings are quite frequent, but a few apparitions have appeared often enough to become famous. From all reaches of the world, here are some of the most well-known spooks.

Facing Page: Ghostslayer by Don Maitz. *Below:* The 1936 photo of the Brown Lady of Raynham Hall.

The Greek Ghost

One of the earliest known ghost stories was told by the Greek philosopher Athenodorus in 40 B.C. On his first night in a haunted house, the ghost of a chain-clad old man appeared. At first Athenodorus ignored the specter, but when the clatter continued, he turned to look at the mysterious ghost, who gestured toward a courtyard. The philosopher followed the ghost outside and watched as the shimmering image vanished while pointing to a spot in the garden. The next day, the area was dug up, revealing a corpse wrapped in chains. After the remains were cremated, the ghost was never seen again.

The Brown Lady of Raynham Hall

The beautiful Lady Dorothy Walpole died in 1726 due to smallpox. At least, that was the *official* cause of death. Others say it was from a broken neck after being pushed down the grand staircase in her home, Raynham Hall in Norfolk, England. Over time, she has made several ghostly appearances on those very stairs, always dressed in a brown gown. Her most famous appearance was captured on film in 1936. Although the photo appears genuine, it is believed that a light leak in the camera may have caused the mysterious image. Of course, that does not explain the many other encounters people have had over the years with the infamous Brown Lady.

Freddy Jackson-Mechanic

In 1919, the United Kingdom's Royal Air Force photographed a squadron of 200 World War I survivors—plus one ghost. Standing in the background is Airman Freddy Jackson, a mechanic who was tragically killed by a spinning propeller two days before the photo was taken. His funeral took place just before the group gathered for the picture. As an official photo, neither the negative nor the prints were altered to include Jackson. It could be argued that anyone could have stepped into the shot, but what is odd is that several members of the squadron recognized Jackson's face.

Above: A photo of a World War I Royal Air Force squadron. It is believed that the ghost of Freddy Jackson stands behind the fourth man in from the left, back row. Detail of the ghostly face is shown behind the man in the circle.

Below: A famous "spirit photograph." In the 1870s, William Mumler combined photos to create this print of Mary Todd Lincoln with the ghostly image of her husband Abraham Lincoln and one of their sons.

Abraham Lincoln

Many phantoms appear to have taken up residence in the White House in Washington, D.C. One of the most famous is the ghost of Abraham Lincoln. Murdered in 1865, the former president is said to wander the halls and rooms of the White House. In particular, his spirit appears in what is today the Lincoln Bedroom. When Lincoln lived, this room was his personal office. One sighting described the phantom president standing with hands clasped behind his back, looking out the window. Another witness saw him sitting on his bed, putting on his boots. While staying in the White House in the 1940s, Queen Wilhelmina of the Netherlands answered a late-night knock at her door. The ghost of Lincoln stood in the hallway. Or so she claimed.

Above: Lincoln's Last Day by Howard Pyle. Many people claim to have seen the ghost of the former president in the White House.

Sad Lads

There are many reports of young ghosts—all with sad tales of early deaths. Perhaps they did not want to leave Earth at such a young age. Or perhaps the ghosts were merely hallucinations, seen by people who wished their dead friends and relatives were still alive.

Willie Lincoln

Young Willie Lincoln, the son of President Abraham Lincoln, was 11 years old when he died of typhoid fever in 1862. His father was heartbroken. In later years, after the president's assassination in 1865, reports surfaced of ghosts running in the halls of the White House, accompanied by the sound of child-like giggling. Some say the president finally reunited with his son, enjoying time that they didn't have while on Earth.

Above: William Wallace Lincoln.

Blue Boy of Gettysburg College

After the Civil War ended in 1865, several orphanages were set up to provide homes for children whose fathers had died in the war. In Gettysburg, Pennsylvania, one such orphanage was run by Rosa Carmichael, a woman who abused the children in her care. One winter, a young boy is said to have escaped, running to nearby Gettysburg College. He was taken in by the women who lived in Stevens Hall. When the school's headmistress arrived, the women hurriedly opened the window and hid the boy on the outside ledge. It took some time before the headmistress left, and when the ladies ran to open the window, the boy was no longer there. Some time after that, residents reported sightings of a young boy, face blue with cold. The Blue Boy still appears today, although what really happened to the young man has never been discovered.

Facing Page: Fault Lines by Don Maitz. A ghost helps a young boy.

THE FOX SISTERS

Margaret and Kate Fox were 12 and 10 years old when their home in Hydesville, New York, became the center of ghostly activity. In early spring, 1848, the family started hearing strange knocking sounds, which seemed to be coming from inside the walls. Sometimes it sounded like furniture was being rapped on. The family suspected a ghost was causing the noise. On March 31, the youngest sister, Kate, tried to communicate with the unseen tapper. She snapped her fingers several times, and then challenged the ghost to repeat the sounds. To everyone's amazement, the spirit mimicked her snapping noises. Years later that day would be called the birth of spiritualism, the ability to talk to the dead.

Below: The Fox family hears odd tapping sounds in their home.

The tapping returned regularly. Many people heard the sounds. The two girls acted as mediums, which are contacts to the spirit world. The "Hydesville Rappings" and the Fox Sisters became famous. Their older sister, Leah Fox Fish, joined the girls. She also acted as their business manager. She had them conduct public performances of their skills as mediums at meetings in the area.

P.T. Barnum, the famous showman, brought the Fox sisters to New York City, where the girls performed séances. They profited nicely from their spirit connections. Rich and poor alike believed in Margaret and Kate's powers. However, there were many skeptics. The only problem was that no one could figure out how the tapping occurred. The Fox sisters seemed to be the real thing.

Above: The Fox Sisters: Margaret, Kate and Leah.

Finally, on October 21, 1888, more than 40 years after it had all begun, Margaret Fox gave a lecture at New York's Academy of Music. Sitting on a small pine platform before an audience of 2,000, Margaret proceeded to snap her big toe joint—and it sounded just like the spirit tapping. She could even direct the sound to different parts of the theater. The fraud was finally exposed.

By this time, however, many people claimed to be true mediums. Spiritualism had found a foothold, and to this day, people continue to wonder whether it's real or fake.

POLTERGEIST ADVICE

Poltergeists are supernatural beings that like to be noticed. They may make loud noises: knocks, taps, moans, or creaks. They move objects: furniture, books, and sometimes even toys. But do poltergeists, or "noisy ghosts," really exist? Most have proven to be the work of the living. Some of their frightening pranks have even turned into successful horror movies. However, there are some strange happenings that have yet to be explained.

Toys "R" Us

Some say the Sunnyvale, California, Toys "R" Us toy store is host to a ghost. The store's poltergeist scatters toys and books, sends objects flying, and even calls out to people. In 1978, psychic Sylvia Brown spent a night in the store. She learned that the poltergeist was a man by the name of Johan Johnson, who died in 1884—right on a spot where the store now sits. Many investigations have

Above: A photo from the haunted toy store. Is the ghost of Johan Johnson in the photograph?

been conducted over the years at the haunted location, but Toys "R" Us does not want Johan to leave. When stories of his activities are reported, lots of people come to the store!

Bell Witch

For many years in the early 1800s, John Bell and his family reportedly experienced a Tennessee poltergeist's nastiness. The entity knocked, whispered, pulled off bed covers, yanked hair and slapped faces. In 1819, reports of the "Bell Witch" reached Nashville, Tennessee. Andrew Jackson, future president and hero of the War of 1812, heard the ghost stories. Interested, he traveled to the Bell farm intending to drive away the evil spirit, or to prove it a hoax. But the Bell Witch terrorized Jackson, and he left within two days. He was quoted as saying, "I'd rather fight the British in New Orleans than to have to fight the Bell Witch." Years later, John Bell died, reportedly poisoned by the Bell Witch. It does seem odd, however, that in all those years, the Bell family never simply moved away.

Above: The Bell house.

Left: Carney Bell, the great-great-great-great grandson of John Bell, is shown by the historic marker in Adams, Tennessee, that tells the story of the Bell Witch. Bell is wearing the period clothes he wears when he portrays John Bell.

SCHOOL SPIRITS

"We've got spirit, yes we do!
We've got spirit, how 'bout you?!"

This popular school cheer fits nearly every college and university in the world, not just because students support their teams, but also because nearly all places of higher learning seem to have at least one resident ghost. There are thousands of reports of ghostly activities in schools. Common haunts include eerie dorms, classrooms, halls, theaters, attics, and basements. From stories of unhappy students who died at school to wandering spectral teachers, colleges seem filled with both the living and the dead.

Some say there is a good reason for so much activity in schools. Poltergeists reportedly draw their energy from unhappy teenagers. Of course, if people weren't happy at school, why would they stay there after death?

In New Hampshire's Keene State College, Harriet Huntress reportedly haunts the dorm bearing her name: Huntress Hall. Weird noises often come from the attic.

Facing Page: Dispell Magic by Don Maitz. *Below:* A June 1923 photo of a spooky, mist-covered lane behind the University of Toronto, Ontario.

Canada's University of Toronto is fond of Burt, the dedicated caretaker of the school's theater. The only problem is that Burt has been dead for many years. But that hasn't stopped him from going to work in his blue uniform, which is seen as a sky-colored haze that sometimes hovers in the lobby. Burt is even credited with once preventing an electrical fire from spreading by alerting the theater's managing director.

GHOST GUESTS

Above: Sarah Winchester.

Ghosts are notorious for inhabiting hotels and homes. One of the most well-known ghostly haunts is the Winchester Mystery House in San Jose, California. In the mid-1800s, the Winchester family made a fortune through the sale of rifles, many of which were used during the American Civil War. When William Winchester died of tuberculosis in 1881, his wife Sarah inherited a fortune of over $20 million dollars, plus nearly half of the company's stock.

After her husband's death, Sarah's life was empty. Her only child had died shortly after birth, and with her husband gone, she became very lonely. A friend suggested that she speak to a medium, who claimed to have the ability to talk to the dead. During a séance, the medium reportedly contacted William Winchester, who warned Sarah that the thousands of spirits whose lives had been ended by Winchester rifles had cursed their family. Sarah was told that she needed to start a new life and build a home for herself and all those fallen spirits. As long as she kept building the house, she would live. When she stopped, she would die.

In 1884, Sarah purchased 62 acres of land in San Jose, California. For the next 38 years, she kept carpenters, plumbers and craftsmen working on a very unusual Victorian mansion.

Above: A view of the Winchester house's tower, destroyed in a 1906 earthquake.

Although beautifully constructed with all the most modern conveniences, the odd house was filled with mazes designed to confuse bad spirits. She created stairs that led nowhere, chimneys that stopped partway up, and doors that opened to empty space. By the time Sarah finally died in her sleep on September 4, 1922, the massive home had 160 rooms.

Above: Sarah Winchester designed a house filled with oddities. Here are stairs leading to nowhere.

Today, the house is a California historical landmark, open for tours. Not surprisingly, many ghostly encounters have been reported. But is it any wonder that odd things happen in such an oddly built house? Or is Sarah still there, watching over her mansion?

Above: The exterior of the Winchester mansion. Today, the house is known as the Winchester Mystery House. It is a California historical landmark, open for tours.

SHRIEKS AT SEA

There's no natural law that says ghosts must stay on land. Many spooks haunt shipboard decks, engine rooms, ballrooms, and staterooms. Even areas of the sea where tragedies have occurred reportedly echo with the voices of the dead. The creaks and grinds of mighty ships may be caused by their steel construction… or some tragic souls whose spirits remain forever at sea.

The *Queen Mary*

The ocean liner *Queen Mary* was a British ship launched in 1934. It was one of the largest passenger ships of its time, measuring 1,019 feet (311 m) from bow to stern. It had more than 1,500 passenger cabins, plus a crew of about 1,100.

In 1940, during World War II, the *Queen Mary* was used for military service. The ship was given a coat of grey camouflage paint. "The Grey Ghost" became a troopship, transporting soldiers across the Atlantic Ocean. On October 2, 1943, as it traveled just off the coast of Ireland, the *Queen Mary* accidentally crossed paths with a small escort ship called the HMS *Curacoa*. The *Curacoa* was sliced in half, killing more than 300 crewmen.

In 1974, a television crew was on a boat that passed directly over the spot where the *Queen Mary* and the *Curacoa* collided. As they sailed over the icy waters of the tragic location, the

Below: A ghostly-looking *Queen Mary* sails out of New York amidst heavy fog.

camera crew recorded strange pounding noises. Did the eerie sounds come from the ghosts of those long-dead sailors? In the years since, others have reported terrifying sounds and voices in those same haunted waters.

Today, the *Queen Mary* is a hotel and restaurant, docked in Long Beach, California. It makes

Above: The *Queen Mary,* permanently docked, still has reports of ghostly activities.

no secret of its on-board ghosts. The spectral figure of a crewman, accidentally crushed by watertight door #13, has been spotted below decks. The first-class swimming pool also sports ghostly activity, with wet footprints and splashing noises when the pool area is supposedly empty. Plus, several of the ship's staterooms are home to ghostly sightings and unexplained noises.

The USS *Hornet*
As with any aircraft carrier, the USS *Hornet* is a dangerous place to work. Over the years more than 300 people died aboard this tragedy-soaked ship. Besides dying

Above: The USS *Hornet,* an aircraft carrier with a proud and tragic history.

from war injuries, many sailors have been sucked into air intakes, blown off the deck, or walked into spinning propellers. On several occasions, crewmen were killed by super-heated 1,500-degree F (815 C) steam erupting out of pipes leading to the engine. Today, the *Hornet* is docked at the US Naval base in Alameda, California. Visitors and staff have sometimes reported meeting spectral sailors who seem to work, talk, drop tools, open and close hatches, flush toilets, and continue to carry out their ghostly orders.

SCARES IN THE AIR

Ever since people started flying in airplanes in the early 20th century, there have been reports of spirits in the sky. Military and commercial airlines alike have been haunted by high-flying ghosts. Stories include spectral pilots, passengers, mechanics, and even phantom planes. Ghosts have reportedly made airplane repairs, sent warnings, and pulled pranks, but at least these traveling ghouls get to fly for free.

Phantom Spitfire

The Spitfire is considered one of the finest fighter planes of World War II. In Kent, England, the town of Biggin Hill was a Spitfire station for a number of Royal Air Force squadrons. Germany's Luftwaffe (air force) bombed it repeatedly, but the station continued operating throughout the war years. Today, a phantom Spitfire reportedly circles the skies over Biggin Hill, its engines roaring. Is it possible the phantom plane is hauntingly protecting its homeland?

Below: World War II fighter pilot Johnny Checketts sits in his Spitfire at Biggin Hill, England in 1943.

Continental Aircraft #886

"Help me. I'm cold." A woman's whispered message came across a Continental Airlines intercom phone at 2:00 A.M. A flight attendant dutifully moved toward the rear of the plane, where the call had originated. But after pulling back the dividing curtain, she found all her passengers in their seats, fast asleep—no one had used the phone. This incident might have been chalked up to a passenger pulling a prank, except that it happened more than once. Did they have a ghostly victim needing a blanket? Or was it a sleepwalking frequent flyer?

Above: A Continental Airlines flight in the air.

HAUNT HUNTERS

The immensely popular 1984 movie *Ghostbusters* featured ghost-hunting professors who "bust" New York City specters using ectoplasm-capturing proton guns. These unique proton packs were actually the work of Columbia Pictures' prop department, but real-life ghost hunters have their own list of don't-leave-home-without-it equipment.

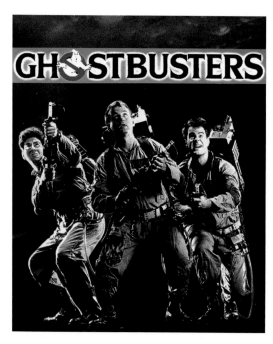

Above: The 1984 movie *Ghostbusters* featured its heroes using ectoplasm-capturing proton guns.

Electromagnetic Field (EMF) Meter
Your body may be trying to tell you something: your skin registers a sudden drop in temperature, a shudder travels through you, or your hairs stand on end. You think you're in the presence of a ghost, but how can you be sure? With an electromagnetic field meter, ghost hunters say they can confirm the presence of spirits. The EMF meter measures a ghost's electrical energy. However, experienced ghost hunters point out that it's important to learn what the meter readings actually mean. Many readings come from everyday sources like televisions, appliances, or even electrical wires.

Temperature Sensing Equipment
Specter searchers use thermometers and thermal scanners to find "cold spots"—sudden or extreme temperature changes in a certain area. A cold spot may be a ghost appearing.

Thermal Imaging Scope
A step above the basic equipment, a thermal imaging scope uses infrared technology to let you see the shape and size of a cold mass detected by a thermal scanner.

Motion Detector
If you know nothing else should be around, a motion detector can be a great device to alert you to movement in a room or hallway. Of course, it will also detect bugs, animals, and other ghost hunters.

Compass

A compass—the needle kind, not an electronic one—will react to magnetic or electrical forces, acting as a pointer to ghostly activity. Of course, it can also be used to help ghost hunters find their way if they've become lost in a strange place.

Camera

Any kind of camera will help prove your ghost stories are true, but a 35mm camera loaded with black and white or infrared film may be the best bet when trying to capture a ghostly presence.

Digital Audio Recorder

An audio recording of ghostly sounds can be used to determine whether you heard naturally occurring sounds or an electronic voice phenomenon.

There are also a number of basic items recommended by ghost hunters. A watch, pen, and a notebook allow you to describe a supernatural event and record exactly when it occurred. For basic safety and communication, it's also a good idea to have flashlights, extra batteries, a first-aid kit, and walkie-talkies or mobile phones. But many ghost hunters insist that the most important item to bring is an open mind.

Below: In 1996, ghost hunter Andrew Green, once dubbed "Britain's Spectre Inspector," displays some technical equipment.

Specter Skeptic

Are you able to talk to spirits? Do you know a ghost on a first-name basis? Do you want to earn $1 million the easy way? Magician James Randi, also known as "The Amazing Randi," has offered to pay $1 million to anyone who can prove any psychic, supernatural, or paranormal ability, under proper scientific testing conditions.

The James Randi Educational Foundation (JREF) has the money ready and waiting—and it's been waiting for decades. The challenge began in 1964, during a live radio show, when Randi scoffed at anyone who claimed to have psychic abilities. The skilled magician thought it was all trickery. A parapsychologist challenged him to "put his money where his mouth is." Randi agreed on the spot, offering $1,000 of his own money to anyone who could prove paranormal power under observational conditions. The challenge has since grown to today's sum of $1 million. Between 1997 and February 2005, 360 official applications arrived at JREF. No one has been able to collect the prize money.

In 1972, Randi made headlines again, challenging popular psychic Uri Geller's claims that he possessed supernatural powers. Experienced magicians could easily duplicate Geller's abilities to bend spoons. Geller, however, insisted that his abilities were not tricks, but legitimate psychic powers. Randi repeated his challenge, asking Geller to undergo controlled tests to prove psychic ability. Geller never accepted Randi's challenge.

Maybe ghosts don't like to be tested. Perhaps ghosts are real, or maybe they're fake. Belief in ghosts and the paranormal varies from person to person. Ancient Chinese scholar and writer Zhu Xi may have best summed up a person's belief or disbelief in ghosts: "If you believe it, there will be, but if you don't, there will not."

Above: Famous skeptic and professional magician James Randi. He established the James Randi Educational Foundation (JREF), which will award $1 million to anyone who can prove paranormal power under controlled conditions. Although several hundred people have signed up, no one has ever collected the money.

GOBLINS

Many people think ghosts and goblins go together like bread and butter, but they are actually two distinct types of beings. Unlike airy, supernatural ghosts, goblins are very much part of our physical world. These nasty little creatures are human in shape but much smaller in size. They have horrific, deformed faces, often with eyes that glow red.

Goblins are closely related to brownies, the helpful creatures of Celtic myths. They sometimes perform household chores, such as sweeping floors or churning milk into butter. But goblins are also notorious troublemakers. If angered, they tip over pails of milk, or blow soot down chimneys. They also commit more sinister deeds.

Goblins come from the folktales of France. According to the stories, the first goblins emerged from the Pyrenees Mountains of southwestern France, which is the dividing mountain range between France and Spain. After leaving their mountain homes, hoards of goblins spread rapidly throughout France, then multiplied all over Europe. According to some legends, after infesting Scandinavia, goblins came to the British Isles as stowaways aboard Viking ships.

The native Celtic people of Britain called the invaders *Robin Goblin*, which is how we get the name *hobgoblin* today. As stories of these creatures spread, their reputation became more sinister. The name hobgoblin was shortened to goblin. While hobgoblins sometimes commit playful pranks, true goblins don't hesitate to pull tricks that can do serious harm to people. They also like to torment farm animals, especially horses. If you see a horse snorting and stamping its feet, it's possible the poor beast has a goblin on its back.

There is one proven way to rid a house infested with these terrible creatures. For some reason, goblins are attracted to flax seed. Before you go to bed, spread a large handful of these seeds on the floor. Goblins will have an irresistible urge to pick up and count every single seed. If you repeat this procedure several times, the goblins will finally get so bored that they will leave for good.

Above: Horned King by Don Maitz. Goblins reportedly like to torment farm animals, especially horses. If a horse is snorting and stamping its feet, it's possible that a nasty, red-eyed goblin is sitting on the poor animal's back.

GLOSSARY

APPARITION

A sudden, startling supernatural appearance of a person or thing, such as a ghost, that appears real.

BARNUM, P.T.

Considered the American "master showman," P.T. Barnum (1810-1891) made a fortune putting on countless shows and exhibits featuring unusual people, animals, and wide-ranging curiosities. A zealous promoter, he described the circus he founded as "the greatest show on Earth."

CELTIC

Refers to the people or language of the Celts, who dominated the British Isles and parts of France and Scandinavia for hundreds of years before the Roman invasion and occupation of 43 A.D.

ELECTROMAGNETIC FIELD (EMF)

Electromagnetic fields can be described as invisible lines of force that surround all electrical devices, such as appliances, computers, televisions, power lines, and wiring. Any time an electric current runs through a wire or an appliance, it produces an EMF. EMFs are present everywhere in our daily lives but are invisible to the human eye. Some ghost hunters believe that EMF readings increase in areas where ghosts have been present. It is also thought that ghosts or spirits can manipulate EMFs to move items in the physical world.

HALLUCINATION

A sensory experience of something that does not exist outside the mind. A hallucination can be caused by a disorder of the nervous system or in response to drugs. However, many people may occasionally experience hallucinations just before falling asleep.

INFRARED

Infrared refers to a certain range of electromagnetic radiation. Several technological devices allow infrared radiation to be made visible. Visible infrared waves can show variations in temperature, with hotter objects a different color than cooler things. Ghost hunters may use infrared-sensitive film to photograph "cold spots" that are much cooler than the surrounding air.

MEDIUM

A person who communicates between the Earthly world and the world of spirits. Spirit mediums may work in séances, or, more commonly today, "channel" the thoughts of a dead person when writing articles or books.

PARANORMAL

An experience or perception that is supernatural—that cannot be explained by science.

PARAPSYCHOLOGY

A type of psychology that deals with the investigation of allegedly psychic phenomena, such as mind reading or psychokinesis (the ability to bend objects through mental processes).

PHANTOM

Something that does not actually exist but seems apparent to the senses. A phantom may be the result of a mirage or optical illusion.

POLTERGEIST

Ghosts who make noise and like to make their presence known. "Poltergeist" comes from the German words for "knock" and "spirit."

PSYCHIC

A person with extraordinary perception and understanding of the human mind. A psychic is especially sensitive to supernatural forces and influences.

SÉANCE

A meeting used by a medium to receive spirit communications.

SPECTER

Something apparently seen that is not in the physical world, especially a scary vision.

SPIRIT PHOTOGRAPHY

A trick used by criminals and hoaxers of the early 1900s, in which photographic negatives were altered so that a picture seemed to show ghostlike images. Photography was a new art form, and many believed it was possible for photos to show things the human eye couldn't normally see. People paid large sums of money to have spirit photographs taken in order to contact dead relatives.

SPIRITUALISM

A religious movement, prominent from the 1840s to the 1920s, holding the belief that spirits of the dead could be contacted by mediums. These spirits were believed to be capable of providing guidance in both worldly and spiritual matters.

INDEX

Above: Grim Reaper in Purgatory by Don Maitz.